THE VALUES LIBRARY

CITIZENSHIP

In a democracy, the citizens *are* the government.

THE VALUES LIBRARY

CITIZENSHIP

Jay Schleifer

THE ROSEN PUBLISHING GROUP, INC.

NEW YORK

Published in 1990 by The Rosen Publishing Group, Inc.
29 East 21st Street, New York, NY 10010.

First Edition
Copyright 1990 by The Rosen Publishing Group, Inc.

Printed in Canada

Library of Congress Cataloging-in-Publication Data

Schleifer, Jay.
    Citizenship / Jay Schleifer.
    (The Values library)
    Includes bibliographical references.
    Index.
    Summary: Discusses the rights, duties, and responsibilities of citizens and notes some citizens who "made a difference."
    ISBN 0-8239-1113-6
    1. Citizenship—Juvenile literature. [1. Citizenship.]
I. Title. II. Series.
JF801.S35   1990   89-70126
323.6—dc20   CIP
                                                 AC

C O N T E N T S

THE POWER OF AN IDEA

IT IS A COLD DAY IN NOVEMBER—the first Tuesday of the month. Winter has come early this year. Banks of snow and sheets of ice blanket many cities and towns. Even so, more than 60 million Americans leave the warmth of their homes. They travel many miles. Then they stand in long, slow-moving lines. It is Election Day.

Each voter knows his or her ballot probably will not decide the election. Elections are won by thousands of votes, not by one or two. But to each voter, his or her own vote is very important. Thousands of other people have already worked for months on this election. They put up posters, mailed letters and made phone calls. They gave their time and effort to the candidate or party of their choice. They did this without expecting payment. They did it to help their candidate win. Millions of other people in nations all over the world work hard for their elections, too. What force moves them? What reward do they expect?

It is the worst possible moment for any nation—wartime. At government offices across the land, hundreds of thousands of young people come forward. They pledge to give up their private lives for years. They willingly promise to serve their nation in the fight. They know that many will give their lives. They are still willing to join the armed forces. In times of war, a law does make the young men serve. But there are ways of avoiding it. Those ways have been used by men in other lands facing the same sacrifice.

Citizens have a duty to serve in the armed forces.

And what of the young women who volunteer? No law makes them serve. They do it because they are citizens. And they believe that to be a *citizen* is important. It is worth more than time, or money, or even a risk to life itself.

That is the power of an idea called *citizenship.*

Citizenship is important to people of many lands. Citizens of Canada and Australia, of France and Germany, of Italy and Sweden are proud of their right to vote. People in Poland, in Russia, and in China also believe in democracy. They have stood up against their governments. They have risked their safety. They are willing to fight for the full rights of citizenship.

In this book, we will look at citizenship. We will see where it comes from. We will look at what it means. We will see what happens when it works. We will see what goes wrong when it doesn't. The citizens who believe in their country are what makes any nation work. And as long as people know why citizenship is important, nations will survive. As long as people continue to be good citizens, their nations will always be safe and strong.

WHAT IS CITIZENSHIP?

THE DICTIONARY DEFINES CITIZENSHIP AS "the condition of having the rights, privileges and duties of a citizen."

That is the same as saying, "a singer is someone who can sing," right?

When we look up the definition of *citizen*, we find what we are looking for: A citizen, the word experts tell us, is "a native or naturalized member of a state or nation. He or she owes allegiance to its government and is entitled to its protection."

Native? Naturalized? Owes allegiance? Entitled to protection? What protection? What allegiance? We need to slow down. We need to look at the idea in a logical way. We need to start at the beginning.

The Law of Blood

The earliest form of citizenship began long, long ago. Perhaps even before we could speak, humans already knew one thing. They knew they lived in a dangerous, brutal world. Other creatures were bigger, faster, stronger. Many animals killed humans for food. Great natural forces threatened man's existence. A single storm could wipe out food supplies for weeks or months.

People soon learned that no one could survive alone. Only by joining with others could people be safe. Only in a group could humans live, learn and grow.

The first group was natural—the family. Parents watched over their children, fed them and protected them. In turn, they expected their children's help and loyalty. Nobody called membership in a family "citizenship." But the main ideas were there. These primitive "citizens" worked together to survive all the horrors of life. They gave each other support.

Relatively safe and strong, the family grew in numbers. The larger, new unit became the *tribe.* In most cases, all members of a tribe were related. They came from a common family. That was the basis for membership in the tribe. Today we would call it citizenship.

In those early tribes, you were a member because your parents were members. You had the right to be a citizen because you came from a common family. This is called *citizenship by blood.*

Outsiders might live among the tribe, but they were never part of it. When the tribe controlled an area, only its members had certain rights. Only tribesmen could

The family was the first group in which humans could learn and grow in safety.

own land or property. Only members of the tribe had a voice in making rules and choosing leaders. In other words, you had to be a member of the tribe to be a citizen.

Citizenship by blood still exists in many smaller nations and provinces. And in this century, it was the basis for one of the worst horrors of human history. Adolf Hitler's Nazi party took control of Germany in 1933. Hitler and the Nazis believed that only certain Germans could be citizens. A true German citizen, to Hitler, had to be descended from the ancient Germanic *Aryan* tribes. All other Germans, including millions of Jews, were no longer considered citizens. They lost the rights and protections of citizenship when the Nazis took power. These people had been loyal to Germany for years. They had served their country in war. And now their property, and even their lives, could be taken from them without a trial. Millions were killed or starved. Millions were worked to death as slaves. And these crimes were committed completely within the law! Nazi Germany took civilization back almost to the brutal days at the dawn of history.

The Law of The Soil

Over the years, many tribes split up. Tribesmen went their separate ways. More and more outsiders freely joined existing groups. A time came when the leaders of

In the 1930s, the Nazis
wanted to drive all the
Jews from Germany.

---

growing nations needed a new form of citizenship. A person's original race was no longer as important. The most important part of the new citizenship was loyalty. Everyone who supported the country's king or leader could be a citizen. Loyal citizens received the ruler's protection in return. This was true in ancient Rome.

This new form was *citizenship by soil.* It is a simple idea that has lasted for centuries. If you are born in an area you are a citizen. It doesn't matter whether or not your family is related to the original settlers. This idea was perfect for a world in which people moved around. It worked well in a world where the armies of powerful nations took over other lands. The continent of Europe was like that in the Middle Ages (from 500 AD to about 1500 AD).

From the 1600s to the mid-1900s, one nation, England, succeeded in taking over many other lands. English citizenship was based largely on soil. Thousands of people lived in the British-owned colonies of North America in the 1700s. They were considered British citizens. It didn't matter what land they lived in.

Americans and Canadians today have citizenship by soil. If you are born there, you are a citizen, even if your father or mother came from Europe, or Asia, or anywhere else. Many other nations, too, consider anyone born in the country to be a citizen.

"Subjectship"

The English in the 1700s defined citizenship differently than people do today, however. They called it "subjectship." You owed your allegiance (loyalty) to the king as well as to the nation. More important, the king was your ruler, not your leader. It made no difference whether you liked him or not. Your thoughts about your country were not important. You owed your loyalty to the king until the day one of you died. When your king was dead, you owed your allegiance to his son (or to his daughter if he had no sons).

The American Concept of Citizenship

In the 1770s, there were many British subjects living in the American Colonies. Many of them did not like or agree with the King of England, George the Third. On July fourth in 1776, a group of men did something very brave. They published a paper called *The Declaration of Independence*. It stated, in part: "these Colonies are, of right, and ought to be, free and independent states." The publication of this paper was important. It meant that many citizens wanted America to break its ties with England and her king. Thomas Jefferson, John Adams, and Benjamin Franklin were members of the group. These citizens fought—and won—the Revolutionary War, the war for America's independence.

The Declaration created a new nation. And it created a new kind of citizenship. The new form was called *citizenship by the consent of the governed*. This was truly a new idea. For the first time, the citizens themselves had a choice in how they would be governed. American citizens still owed allegiance to America's government. But it would be a government that they chose. The citizens had the right to vote for their own government. They could change the government's leadership. All they had to do was to exercise their right to vote. The old world, the world of kings, had never seen anything like it.

This form of government is also called *government by contract*. It was established by America's Constitution, the basis for all of the laws of the land. *We choose you to lead*, citizens say to their leaders, *just as you choose to do so. If either of us is ever dissatisfied, the contract is broken. You can quit being a leader anytime you would like. And if we feel you are not right for the job, next election day we can choose someone else.* The contract has worked well. For 200 years America has prospered under this new form of government. And the American democratic system has been widely copied in other lands.

Improvements in the Constitution were needed, to extend the rights of citizenship to all Americans. The Constitution did not outlaw slavery. Only men who owned property could vote. But the Constitution's au-

The Declaration of Independence declared that all men are created equal.

thors provided a system for changes. The 15th Amendment to the Constitution outlawed slavery in 1870. The 19th Amendment gave women the vote in 1920. Improvements continue to be made. Democracy—government by and for the people—continues to be a model for other nations.

In February, 1986, in the Philippines, Corazon Aquino became that country's president. She had won the office in an election against dictator Ferdinand Marcos. He refused to admit the true election results. But the people of the Philippines were behind Aquino. Finally members of the military supported her. Marcos left the Philippines.

Chinese students pro-
tested against their gov-
ernment and were shot in
the streets.

The Philippine people are proud of their new government.

For several years, members of Poland's "Solidarity"
union movement conducted protests. They wanted a
more democratic form of government. In the spring of
1989, elections were finally held in Poland. The Commu-
nist government there had agreed, in part, to the will of
the people.

In June of that same year, students in China demon-
strated for a more democratic form of government. They
felt Chinese communism didn't allow enough personal
freedom.

The students took over Tienanmen Square in the city
of Beijing. They stayed there for many days. They built a
statue right in the square. They called the statue "The
Goddess of Democracy." It looked like America's Statue
of Liberty, another symbol (figure) of democracy.

The Chinese government sent troops to the Square.
Many students were killed. Many more were tried for
crimes against the government. Students who were found
guilty were shot. But the movement for democracy in
China did not die.

The student protesters in China had learned their les-
sons about citizenship. They were willing to make sacrifices for what they believed was right.

The government protects its citizens and their property through the police force.

2

THE RIGHTS AND DUTIES OF CITIZENS

AS WE LEARNED FROM THE DICTIONARY, citizenship developed as an exchange between the people and the government. The people give their loyalty and allegiance to the government. In return the government gives them rights and protection. What does the government do for the people? What does it ask of them in return?

What a Government Does for Its Citizens

No government would remain in power unless it provided certain *rights and protections* for many people. These include:

• *Physical Safety* from enemies near and far. To provide this, governments establish military forces. In times of war, citizens volunteer or are called (drafted) to military service. They serve in the armed forces along with career servicemen and servicewomen.

    • *Public Services:* These include such things as building roads, printing money, and running schools. There are many jobs that affect all the people. It is best if these are done by a single source. It simply would not work if, for example, each family created its own form of money. Governments have traditionally done these jobs.

    • *Protection of Property.* People own property—homes, cars, and other items—which they earn by their labors. Governments ensure that no one can take your property by theft or by force. Many laws protect your property rights.

What Citizens Do for their Governments

    No matter what the form of government, citizens usually have these duties:

    • *To Obey the Law.* This sounds simple, but it is the reason society works. In the United States, for example, there are only two full-time police officers for every 1,000 citizens. Two men could not *force* 1,000 people to obey the law. Citizens are expected to police their own behavior. And by and large they do. People are taught from childhood to obey the law. It is drilled so deeply that most people feel guilty if they do something wrong. Even if no one is watching.

Watch people driving up to a stoplight in the dead of night. They stop and wait, even though there isn't a police car anywhere within miles. Think about how strongly people believe in the idea of simply obeying the law.

• *To Pay Taxes.* The government must pay for the services it provides. Its only source of money is the taxes paid by its citizens. Citizens everywhere complain that their taxes are too high. But they are getting a bargain. Suppose your family had to pay for the cost of the roads leading to your house. You probably couldn't afford it. The job can only be done because the cost is shared. Everyone pays their share when they pay taxes.

• *To Serve in the Armed Forces.* This is the most solemn of the duties of citizens. When the government asks, people put their lives on the line. Good citizens have always been willing to do it. Good citizens think of military service as "the price of freedom."

Good Citizens—Bad Government

Obeying the law, paying taxes and serving in the military when called are the duties of all citizens. But they do not ensure that good government will result. The hardest test of any citizen requires great courage. When a government is wrong, it is the duty of every citizen to speak out.

During the Nazi period the German government committed "crimes against humanity" by killing and enslaving millions of people.

Sometimes action is required to make sure there is change.

Citizens in Nazi Germany were loyal and obedient. They were among the most law-abiding of populations. They paid their taxes and served proudly in the military. Hundreds of thousands gave their lives to protect the ideas of Adolf Hitler. Yet the society created by all these "good citizens" enslaved and killed millions of people. These victims' only "crime" was that they were born as members of the "wrong" race.

Adolf Hitler believed only certain Germans had the right to be citizens. Others, however loyal, had no rights at all. Their property could be taken from them. Even their lives could be taken by the state. In his name the murder of millions of innocent people took place. Others were worked to death as slaves.

When the Nazis lost the war, many Germans felt they had done no wrong! "I followed orders," said one former official after another when they were tried for war crimes. What they were saying was that they were good citizens. And by the standards of Nazi Germany, they were!

We can easily see today what should have happened. Those terrible things could have been prevented. German citizens should have refused to carry out Hitler's orders.

In the United States in the 1960s, many citizens felt their government was wrong. They believed that America should not be fighting a war in Vietnam. This cause appealed to many young people. These young people organized an "anti-war" protest movement.

Many young men refused to register for the draft.

In the 1960s students
protested against the
Vietnam War by burning
their draft cards.

They did not believe that they should serve in the military
in an unjust war. Others burned their draft cards. Others
left the country to live in Canada, or even in Sweden.
There were many protest marches for peace. Thousands
of men and women of all ages spoke out against the
Vietnam war.

Many other Americans believed that the government
was right. They felt American servicemen should fight in
Vietnam. Many young men volunteered to go to Vietnam.
Some were treated badly when they returned. Protesters
accused them of murdering innocent women and children.
Sometimes protesters spat on returning Vietnam veterans.

Both of these groups of Americans felt strongly about
the war. And both groups felt they were being good
citizens. The groups of *active* citizens had something in
common. All of the citizens behaved with the courage of
their convictions. Those young men who volunteered for
duty in Vietnam were willing to give their lives. They
believed the government was right to try to help the Viet-
namese people. Those young men who protested the war
were willing to suffer also. They were willing to go to
prison, or to go into exile (leave the country).

Sometimes the good citizenship of large numbers of
people results in a conflict of ideas. The argument of
each side has some merit. It is through the resolution of

---

these conflicts that democratic governments show hidden strength. Democracy is *flexible*. That means that laws can be changed when ideas change.

All of the active American citizens in the 1960s had something in common. They understood the special responsibilities of good citizenship. They were willing to take action for a cause they believed in.

Other women and men all over the world have been willing to suffer for what they believed was right. Many Russians have protested their government's actions. We call them "dissidents." Dissident is another word for "protester." Many have served long terms in harsh prisons. But their messages have gone out to others around the world. Andrei Sakharov is one of Russia's many famous dissidents. He is a famous scientist. He spoke out against the government. He was sent to prison for his ideas. His work was interrupted when he went to prison. Andrei Sakharov was forced to live in a lonely part of Russia. He had to give up his freedom because he tried to change his country's ideas.

Sometimes the price of good citizenship is very high. Without people willing to make sacrifices, the rights of all citizens are in danger.

3

SPECIAL RESPONSIBILITIES OF GOOD CITIZENSHIP

GOOD CITIZENS OF ANY MODERN NATION obey the law, pay taxes, and serve in the military. But that is not enough. Why not? Because in a democracy WE THE PEOPLE elect the government. *We* are not controlled by a supreme leader or a small group of powerful officials. We are responsible for what our government does.

In a democracy, the people give the orders. If the government does wrong, the people have the power to change it. This difference is like the difference between owning and renting the home you live in. If things don't work, the renter can simply blame the landlord. When you own a home, you *are* the landlord. There is nobody else to blame. To keep things running right, you have to learn how they work. And sometimes you must get your hands dirty to fix things. Sometimes you have to make an effort to keep them in working order.

New citizens take an oath of loyalty to their adopted country.

Learning how your government works is the first step in becoming an effective citizen.

Here are some of the responsibilities we all have as active citizens:

•To Keep Informed

What You Don't Know **Can** *Hurt You.* Some years ago a citizenship education group, The National Council of Social Studies, did some important work. They sent questionnaires to 300 top American leaders. They studied people's opinions about what makes a good citizen. They all agreed on one thing. A good citizen *keeps informed.* All good citizens know what is going on.

Being informed starts in the schools. There you learn your nation's history. There you study the parts of government and what they do. But being informed doesn't end in the schools.

You can find out what is going on in your government. You don't have to look very far or listen very hard. In a democracy, things are argued about loudly and often. People are concerned about war and peace. They discuss how to spend tax money. Neighbors argue about whether their street corner needs a traffic light. Somebody is discussing, debating or arguing about every issue. And somebody else is covering it for the news. You can hear about it on TV. You can read about it in the newspaper. There are often public meetings and hearings, especially on local issues. These meetings are open to all interested citizens.

Good citizens take the time to listen to these discussions. They read, and they keep up with current events. Good citizens listen to both sides of arguments. They get their news from more than one source. Then and only then do they make up their minds.

•To Vote

Your Choice. Once you do make up your mind about a candidate it is time to vote. Voting is one of the most important rights citizens have in a democracy.

In America, the best turnouts are for presidential elections. About 60 percent of Americans eligible to vote show up to cast their ballots for president. In local elections, for town or county government, the total is far less. Voter turnout can be as low as 10 to 20 percent.

Americans are not alone. In most democracies there are many citizens who do not participate. These people can pay a high price for their neglect. The mayor some citizens work to elect may not be honest. She or he may not listen to local citizens with problems.

Decisions of town government usually affect the daily life of a citizen. They can have more impact than anything that happens in the country's capital. The President of the United States, for all his power, cannot help an individual. He can't order the public works department to fix the hole in front of someone's driveway. He or she can't tell the local Board of Education to add a classroom to a school. The mayor, or his or her commissioners, can.

There is a great danger in not voting. An election is going to be held, whether or not the citizens cast their votes. When large numbers of people do not vote, the power in the government passes to the few who do.

An unworthy candidate, backed by a small, well organized group, can get many supporters to the polls. Unless many other citizens exercise the right to vote, such a candidate can gain power for an entire term of office.

In an extreme situation, there is a terrible danger. If few enough citizens care enough to vote, a democracy can die. A government can suspend elections. If there are no protests, the nature of the government can change. A dictatorship can result. German citizens allowed Hitler to come to power after he lost an election.

•To Participate

Work for What You Believe In. Voting is one way to put your citizenship to use. But it is not the only way. You should study important issues and make up your mind about them. Then you have the right to try to help others make up their minds. And you should.

Groups have been set up to influence voters. They are called *political parties.* America has two big ones, the Republicans and the Democrats. Canada's political parties

The major political parties have conventions to nominate their candidates.

Helping to build affordable housing can be a useful volunteer job.

are called the Liberals and the Conservatives. And Canada has a special-interest political party. It concerns itself with the rights of Canadian citizens of French descent. Every democracy has its own political parties. Each political party is a group of citizens. They have banded together to elect candidates. They work together in support of issues they believe in.

Political parties welcome young people who want to join. The work can be hard. But it can be fun.

Helping to elect a candidate takes effort. Some volunteers type. Some answer telephones. Some run computers to send out mailings. Some give out leaflets in shopping centers.

Sometimes volunteers call people to remind them to vote. Other volunteers make sure the elderly can get to the voting places. They can also babysit while parents go to vote.

In the long run, this work is very rewarding. You are helping to decide the future of your city. Or your state. Or even your nation. Look in the phone book. Then stop in and visit your local political club.

You can also join with other groups—or work on your own—for hundreds of other causes. You can help education. You can seek humane treatment of animals. In a democracy, good citizens make their ideas known. They are willing to work hard for what they believe in.

Sometimes one person can make a big difference. One person can make the lives of other people much better.

If your super doesn't sweep the hallway, you can borrow a broom and do it yourself. All your neighbors will feel better about where they live. You can help an elderly neighbor clean house. You can shop for someone who is ill, or cook them a good meal.

If you get together with friends, you can do even more. You can volunteer through your church. You can get some help from a teacher at school. A minister or teacher can help you get organized. If you have an interest in music, or the performing arts, you can do something important. You can sing or dance for patients in hospitals. That kind of fun makes people feel better. You can perform in nursing homes. You can bring happiness to children who are ill.

With help from an adult volunteer, you can do many things. You and your friends can start a garden in an empty lot. A teacher or youth worker can help you get started. It is hard work to make flowers or vegetables grow. It takes sweat, and a lot of time. But you can bring beauty to your neighborhood. And you can bring spirit to your community.

4

CITIZENS WHO MADE A DIFFERENCE

IN THE LAST CHAPTER WE SAID THAT ONE OF THE DUTIES of every citizen is to work for what you believe in. Here are the stories of four citizens who did just that. Each, in his or her own way, advanced citizenship and made it an even more valuable right. These special citizens are:

Thomas Jefferson   •   Harriet Tubman

Mohandas K. Gandhi   •   Terry Fox

Thomas Jefferson—The Inventor of a New Citizenship

In the early 1960s, President John F. Kennedy gave a dinner for some of the brightest people in the land. He looked out over the group of professors and scientists. "This is the greatest collection of mental power ever assembled in the White House," he said "since Thomas Jefferson dined alone."

41

There's never been an American citizen quite like
Jefferson. He was handsome, educated, talented, powerful and rich. There was no reason why he would
want to change anything in his life. There was no
reason for him to risk anything that he had. When
Jefferson was 33, he made an important decision. And
he took action for what he believed. He wrote, and
signed with other patriots, the Declaration of Inde-

Thomas Jefferson,
America's third president,
was the author of the
Declaration of Independ-
ence.

pendence. Had he been captured by the British, these acts would have cost him his life.

Why did he get involved? Because to Jefferson, the main ideas behind British "subjectship" were wrong. No leader had the right to rule just because he was born to a royal family. People had the right to have a say in how they were governed. No one was born better than anyone else. "All men," he wrote, "are created equal." Those are the most important words in the American Declaration of Independence.

Governments, Jefferson felt, were invented by the people to protect and serve. "Kings are the servants of their people, not their owners," he wrote. Thomas Jefferson was one of the inventors of a new kind of government. He was one of the inventors of a new idea of citizenship. A democracy is a government in which people obey the laws. But they also have a voice in how the nation is run.

Jefferson was America's third President. He served two terms, from 1801-1809. Highlights of his presidency include the Louisiana Purchase and the Lewis and Clark Expedition. Lewis and Clark explored and charted much of the Northwest. Jefferson died on the Fourth of July, 1826. He died 50 years to the day after the signing of his Declaration of Independence.

Harriet Tubman helped
slaves escape to the North
through the "Underground
Railroad."

Harriet Tubman—Righting a Great Wrong

American "founding fathers" had been men of high
ideals. But their ideals were not high enough. They had
refused to right a great wrong in the new nation of America. Half a million Africans lived in slavery in the South.
They had no more rights than a horse, a barn, or any
other piece of property. The new constitution mentioned
them only as "three-fifths persons." The number of Rep-
resentatives to the new Congress was based on popula-
tion. Every five slaves were counted as three people.

Slaves—human beings—could be bought and sold.
Some slaves refused to accept that destiny. One was
Harriet Tubman.

Tubman was born into slavery. She escaped to the
free states of the North. She was uneducated and very
poor. But the idea of freedom was all-important to her.
Time and again she returned to the South. She helped
other slaves escape. She was a leading "conductor" on
the "Underground Railroad." The "railroad" was a secret
society. Its members guided slaves North to freedom by
night. More than once, Tubman faced capture and probably death. But she always managed to escape with her
precious cargo.

The courage of Harriet Tubman and others like her
inspired others. A powerful anti-slavery movement was

formed in the North. The country fought a Civil War.
The North defeated the South. Slavery ended in America.
But Harriet Tubman did not rest. She worked to improve
the lives of African Americans. Harriet Tubman helped to
establish schools for ex-slaves. She helped care for the
poor and the aged. Harriet Tubman is an example of
good citizenship at its very best.

Mahatma Gandhi led
India to independence
from Great Britain. He
used "nonviolent civil
disobedience."

Mohandas Karamchand ("Mahatma") Gandhi—World Citizen

Gandhi belongs to a special group of people. These people have worked to change their own countries. They have changed the world we live in.

"Mahatma" means "Great Soul." Gandhi was born in India in 1869. He studied law in London. He then went to South Africa. Many other Indians had gone there to work. They were treated badly. Gandhi worked hard in the fight of Indians in South Africa for civil rights.

In his fight in South Africa, Gandhi developed one of the most important tools for social protest. It is used today, and has been used in some of the most difficult struggles in modern times. It is called "nonviolent civil disobedience." It is also called "passive resistance."

Nonviolent civil disobedience has been used by African Americans fighting for civil rights. In the 1960s, civil rights workers "sat in" at "whites only" lunch counters. Before that the south was segregated. That meant that African Americans and others who were not white had to use separate facilities. There were "whites only" schools, restaurants, hotels—even drinking fountains! Civil rights workers sat in at lunch counters all day long, day after day. They did not give up until anyone could sit down and eat wherever they liked.

Gandhi was put in prison in South Africa because of his work for civil rights. When he was released, Gandhi returned to India. His actions helped to get changes in South Africa. His work made a real difference in the treatment of Indians in South Africa.

In India, Gandhi became a political leader. His Congress Party led the fight for India's independence. After World War II, India became its own nation. More than 100 years in the British Empire came to an end.

Terry Fox—Courage That Inspired a Nation

Sometimes an ordinary person becomes a model for others. This kind of an example can be more inspiring than the work of a national leader. Terry Fox became this kind of "unlikely hero."

Terry Fox was born in Winnipeg, Manitoba in Canada in 1958. He grew up in Coquitlan, British Columbia. Terry found out in his late teens that he had cancer. His right leg was amputated above the knee in 1977.

Terry Fox ran 26 miles a
day for 143 days.

Terry Fox saw great suffering in the cancer wards
where he was treated. That suffering inspired him. He
thought of a way that he could help.

Terry Fox had been an athlete before his cancer. He
decided to use his gift to raise money for cancer research.
Fox trained for 15 months. Then, in April of 1980, he
began what he called his "Marathon of Hope."

Terry Fox started in St. John's, Newfoundland. His
goal was to run across the entire country of Canada. Fox
averaged nearly 26 miles (a regulation marathon run)
every day for 143 days. He ran through snow, hail and
intense heat. He covered more than 3,300 miles.

In September of 1980 Terry Fox learned his cancer had
spread to his lungs. His "marathon" was over. Ten
months later, in 1981, cancer took Terry Fox's life.

Terry Fox's "Marathon of Hope" had raised over 25 million dollars for cancer research. He had been awarded
the Order of Canada, that nation's highest honor. A run
to raise money for cancer research is held in Canada
every year. It is named for Terry Fox.

The world will not forget what this one citizen did for
his fellow human beings. His is the kind of action that
serves as an example for good citizens everywhere.
There is *always* something you can do to help. You need
only to be determined to make a difference.

5

"THE MAN WITHOUT A COUNTRY"

IT IS NOT EASY TO EXPLAIN THE POWER OF CITIZENSHIP. It takes
more than just talking about laws and rights and history.
Sometimes it takes a good story, one that touches the
heart. A minister named Edward Everett Hale wrote
such a story in the mid-1800s. It was called "The Man
Without a Country." The story first appeared as a maga-
zine article. Many people talked about it. They wanted
to read it and reread it. Thousands of copies were printed
in book form.

The book's plot is simple. The title character is Philip
Nolan. He is a young officer in the United States Army.
He meets and joins forces with Aaron Burr. Burr was a
real-life traitor. He planned to set up his own government
in the Western Territories. The plan failed. Burr escaped,
but Nolan was captured and put on trial.

50

The judge knew that Nolan was young and foolish, not really evil. Chances were good that Nolan would get off with a light sentence. But in a moment of anger Nolan cried out. He said he was sick and tired of hearing about what he did to the United States. "I wish to never hear of the United States again!" he declared.

The judge knew exactly what sentence to fit to Nolan's crime. Nolan was banished to live out his life on Navy ships. He was forbidden ever to hear of his native land again. For the rest of his days, he was to be a man without a country.

At first, young Nolan laughed off the sentence. Surely there were worse fates. He would live a life of cruising to interesting ports. He would enjoy life at sea. The court ordered that Nolan be treated kindly and with great courtesy.

But whenever he appeared on board ship, the sailors stopped speaking of home. His newspapers had all articles about America clipped out. Even his uniform lacked the buttons that carry the letters "U.S." They called him "Plain Buttons."

Each ship completed its year or two of cruising to foreign lands and headed home. Nolan was transferred to another outward bound ship. In time, the government forgot Philip Nolan.

One day, his ship freed a cargo of Africans bound for
slavery. They were asked where they wanted to be taken.
The Africans wanted only to be returned to their own land.
The captain told them that their wish to return home was
granted. They shouted with joy. This was more than

52

Alexander Solzhenitzen
was forced to leave Russia
because he criticized the
government.

Nolan's emotions could stand. He revealed his thoughts to a young friend. He longed for America with all his heart.

"Youngster," he said, "if you are ever tempted to say a word or do a thing that shall put a bar between you and your family, your home and your country, boy, pray God that instant to take you home to his own heaven."

Nolan died shortly after. Shipmates entered his cabin to collect his belongings. They were shocked. His small bed was surrounded by a tattered U.S. flag and other symbols of the land he loved—and lost.

Alexander Isayevich Solzhenitzen is another "man without a country." He is a Soviet writer. He used his talents to expose the harsh way the Soviets treated its dissidents (people who speak out and work for reform).

Solzhenitzen wrote a book called *The Gulag Archipelago*. It is named for the hard, cold prison community he was sent to by the government.

Solzhenitzen's work has been translated into many languages. It has been read by people all over the world. Because he criticized the government by telling the truth, Solzhenitzen was exiled. His government forced him to leave Russia.

Solzhenitzen went to Switzerland in 1974. In 1976 he moved to the United States. Solzhenitzen was forced to give up his beloved homeland. In a way he, too, is a "man without a country."

Love of country is an important part of citizenship for everyone everywhere. Not all countries have the same form of government. Governments differ just like languages and customs do.

Many people who love their homelands think everyone should live as they do. But we must all remember that our way may not be best for everyone. Even if we are happy the way we are, others can live differently and be happy too.

Being a good "world citizen" means respecting the rights of other governments as well as those of other people.

When governments are cruel and unjust it is the duty of citizens of the country, and people around the world, to speak out and to work for change. But that is different from simply wanting every country to be just like your own.

Sometimes people who live where the government is harsh and cruel are able to leave. They take their families and start a new life elsewhere. These people are called "immigrants."

The United States is often called "a nation of immigrants." In the early part of the century many people came seeking a better life for themselves and their families. Canada has also benefited from immigrants. New people bring new skills and ideas. They also bring new food, music, and expressions which enrich their new country. Sometimes, the natives of the country are unwilling to accept the new people. They say they are "strange." Good citizenship means helping other people to get along.

Working in a soup kitchen that feeds the homeless is one way of contributing to your community.

6

THE FUTURE OF CITIZENSHIP

THIS BOOK BEGAN WITH LEARNING ABOUT CITIZENSHIP. We started with the dawn of man on earth. We traveled through the age of kings and on to the present day. We have seen what can happen when citizens simply obey the law and follow orders. We have learned why just doing those things is not enough for *our* kind of citizenship. The stories of Thomas Jefferson and Harriet Tubman, Mohandas Gandhi and Terry Fox are important examples for us. We have learned how outstanding citizens can change their country's history. We learned from the fictional story of Philip Nolan. We can see how much citizenship is worth having. We understand what can happen when we take our rights as citizens for granted.

There is a lot of information
available to people in a
free society. A good citizen keeps informed.

Now we can look forward to the future. Here are the challenges that await you, the adult citizen of the 21st century:

•***Keeping Informed***: Knowing what is right and who is right is getting harder and harder. Candidates for office have discovered the power of TV advertising. People running for political office are sold like bread or new cars. Ads have fancy photos and slick slogans. But they don't say much about what the candidates stand for. It will be your job to cut through the flash and find the truth. Ask questions.Read many resources. Learn all you can. The leaders you elect are the leaders you will have to live with.

Too often citizens in a democracy are lazy. They take their rights for granted. They leave to others the job of making things better for everyone. They do not participate in politics or community service. You can help to change that.

At the very least, vote! Vote in every election. But also be aware of chances to help. You can make your city, state and nation better places to live. There are countless challenges. We must take care of our planet. We should help the poor and the homeless. We need to help the government fight against crime and drugs. Do your part!

As a society grows, changes become necessary. How these changes affect everyone is often up to the govern-

ment. Concerned citizens can monitor changes. They can make sure new laws are just.

Concerned citizens can help other citizens stay informed. They can take action to call attention to a problem. They can follow up as a group until a problem is solved.

Good citizens care about their country and their fellow citizens. They are willing to work hard to make things better for everyone. If we were all good citizens, this would be a wonderful world.

You can help to make the world better. We've shown you how to get started. Now it is up to you to do your part.

Glossary: *Explaining New Words*

allegiance Loyalty or devotion to a nation, government, person, group or cause.

amendments Added sections, especially to a contract or agreement.

ballot A paper on which a vote is marked.

banished Thrown out of a society or group and not allowed to return.

billion A thousand million.

candidate A person desiring a job, position or government office.

citizen A member of a state or nation. A citizen owes allegiance to the government and receives its protection and rights under the law.

citizenship The condition of being a citizen.

citizenship by blood Being a citizen because your parents or family were citizens.

citizenship by soil Being a citizen because you were born in a certain area.

government by contract An arrangement in which leaders choose to lead and citizens choose to let them. Either group can change its mind.

immigrant A person who settles permanently in a foreign country.

influence The ability to change people's views or decisions.

income tax Money paid to the government by its citizens to help pay for government services.

issue A question under discussion.

naturalization The legal process of making a foreigner, (also called an alien) a citizen.

naturalized Made a citizen by legal process.

obedience Following orders or instructions. Doing what is ruled or required. Carrying out one's responsibilities.

political party A group of like-minded people who work together to choose candidates and get them elected.

subjectship A kind of citizenship in which one owes allegiance to a king or ruler as well as a nation.

tribe A group of people living together and usually born of a common family.

"underground railroad" A secret society that helped slaves to escape from the South before the Civil War.

For Further Reading

Adams, John R. *Edward Everett Hale.* Boston: Twayne Publishers, 1977. A complete biography of the author of "The Man Without a Country". Covers Hale's career on the pulpit as well as his writings.

Brewer, David J. *American Citizenship.* New Haven: Yale University Press, 1914. One of the Yale lecture series on citizenship. Brewer stresses the virtues of character and service in good citizens.

Hockin, Thomas A. *Government In Canada (Comparative Modern Government Series, Illustrated),* 1976, Norton. This book discusses the basics about becoming a Canadian citizen and how the Canadian government is organized.

Kottner, James H. *The Development of American Citizenship:1608-1870.* Chapel Hill, N.C.: University of North Carolina Press, 1978. A winner of the Jamestown Prize for American History, Kottner describes how citizenship changed and grew throughout the colonial, revolutionary, and civil war periods.

Kramer, Lloyd S., ed. *Paine and Jefferson on Liberty.* New York: Continuum Publishing Co., 1988. A well edited selection of speeches and writings by two of America's most celebrated citizens and patriots.

Maxson, Charles H. *Citizenship.* New York: Oxford University Press, 1930. An historical look at how citizenship developed from early cultures to the present.

Morgan, Joy Elmer, ed. *The American Citizen's Handbook,* 6th Edition. Washington: National Council for the Social Studies, 1968. Discusses the role of the American citizen in full detail; also includes many patriotic songs, poems and historical detail.

Vincent, William S. *Roles of the Citizen.* Evanston, Ill.: Row Peterson & Co., 1959. A textbook on citizenship, covering every aspect of the process.

INDEX

About the Author

A native of New York, Jay Schleifer received his B.A. from City College of New York. He taught for five years in the New York City school system, with an emphasis on Special Education. He was editor for five years of *Know Your World*, a high/low classroom periodical. He is the author of five high/low books and was a development editor for Field Publications, in Middletown, Connecticut.

Photo Credits and Acknowledgments

Cover Photo: Stephanie FitzGerald
Pages 2,7,11,20,30-31,32,39,56,59, Stephanie FitzGerald; p.19,24,27,36-37,47,48,52,
Wide World Photos; p.17,42, Library of Congress; pg.13 Bettman Newsphotos; pg.45, Culver
Pictures Inc.

Design and Production: Blackbirch Graphics,Inc.

DATE DUE

MEDIALOG INC
ALEXANDRIA KY 41001